1001 Brilliant Writing Ideas

Teaching inspirational story-writing for all ages

Ron Shaw

Routledge
Taylor & Francis Group

LONDON AND NEW YORK

First published 2003 by Curriculum Corporation, Australia
This edition published 2008 by Routledge
2 Park Square, Milton Park, Abingdon, Oxon OX14 4RN

Simultaneously published in the USA and Canada
by Routledge
270 Madison Ave., New York, NY 10016

Routledge is an imprint of the Taylor & Francis Group, an informa business

© 2008 Ron Shaw

Typeset in Garamond and Helvetica by
RefineCatch Limited, Bungay, Suffolk
Printed and bound in Great Britain by
Bell & Bain Ltd, Glasgow

British Library Cataloguing in Publication Data
A catalogue record for this book is available from the British Library

Library of Congress Cataloging in Publication Data
Shaw, Ron
    1001 brilliant writing ideas: teaching inspirational story-writing
for all ages / Ron Shaw.
        p. cm.
    1. English language – Rhetoric – Study and teaching. 2. Creative
writing – Study and teaching. 3. Fiction – Technique. I. Title. II.
Title: One thousand one brilliant writing ideas. III. Title: One
thousand and one brilliant writing ideas.
    PE1404.S514 2008
    808.3'1071—dc22
    2007022719

Artwork by Aja Bongiorno

ISBN10: 0–415–44709–7 (pbk)
ISBN10: 0–203–93720–1 (ebk)

ISBN13: 978–0–415–44709–6 (pbk)
ISBN13: 978–0–203–93720–4 (ebk)

1001 Brilliant Writing Ideas

How often do you hear your pupils cry 'what can I write about?'

1001 Brilliant Writing Ideas offers teachers endless ideas and inventive suggestions, opening up new opportunities for creative writing lessons. With over a thousand different 'story-starters' across a vast range of genres and narrative styles, this versatile book provides food for thought for pupils of a wide range of ages and abilities.

This highly practical and richly illustrated photocopiable resource:

- addresses the 'blank mind' problem, offering pupils a plethora of story-writing ideas and suggestions;
- enables teachers to inspire pupils who struggle with creative writing;
- provides prompts to set ideas into motion, whilst leaving plenty of scope for original and creative thought;
- challenges pupils, encouraging them to use higher-level thinking skills;
- offers mix-and-match stimulus pieces that can be used independently or put together to give pupils more or less support as required.

Any teacher whose inventiveness is flagging, and whose pupils are running out of ideas, will find this an essential classroom resource.

Ron Shaw has many years of classroom experience and is the author of more than forty books helping primary and secondary school students to improve their thinking skills.

Contents

Introduction

It was none other than Roald Dahl who proclaimed that writing stories isn't easy. There are times when ideas won't come, he said. The mind goes blank.

As teachers we are all familiar with the student who 'clams up' in story writing lessons. If we manage to prise two or three sentences from such a child we are doing well.

This book addresses the 'blank mind' dilemma by offering the student a plethora of story-writing ideas and suggestions. Care has been taken to provide equally for boys and girls, allowing for their different interests.

In many instances the student is given prompts, to set ideas into motion. However, there is still a great deal of scope for original and creative thought.

Included in some of the story-writing tasks are additional instructions. Sometimes these instructions may seem to bear little relevance to the story itself. This is deliberate and is designed to:

- assist the student by directing thoughts along certain lines;
- challenge the student by calling upon higher-level thinking skills, involving, for example, the matching of a particular character to a given situation.

The wide variety of themes, together with the range of ideas spread across them, should ensure that all students have plenty to write about.

There is no set way to use this book. One suggestion would be to use Sensational Settings in conjunction with Story Starters or some other page. Another idea could be to mix Charismatic Characters with Tantalising Titles. Either way, a delightful combination of the real with the fanciful could result, bringing a sense of achievement and satisfaction to both the writer and you, the teacher.

Happy and fulfilling writing!

PLEASUREABLE AND PREPOSTEROUS PLOTS TO PONDER 1

Consider the story starters below and then choose one to write about.

Survivor

You are drifting at sea on a life raft, the sole survivor of a shipwreck. Storm clouds are gathering. Land is just visible on the misty horizon. *Describe your adventure from now until you are rescued.*

Oh no!

I thought that drink tasted strange. What's happening to me? Oh no!

Goliath the Gorilla

Goliath was the biggest, meanest, scariest gorilla of them all. He was afraid of nothing. Nothing, that is, except . . . mice!

Harry Hough

His nose is long and green. His hair stands up in spikes. Wispy hairs stick out from each ear. Enormous bushy eyebrows hang out over droopy eyes. This is Harry Hough, who lives in a hole. Who is Harry, and what is his secret?

Money!

It's relaxing sitting under this tree. I watch as a leaf floats to the ground. Then another. And another. But wait . . . they're not leaves . . . it's . . . money!

The Haunted House

I am trapped in a haunted house. There are no lights and it is totally dark. I reach out but all I feel are cobwebs. *Begin by describing your feelings, emotions and thoughts together with any physical symptoms you may be experiencing. Then describe what you hear, if anything. Lastly, tell all that happens as you manage, eventually, to escape to freedom.*

PLEASUREABLE AND PREPOSTEROUS PLOTS TO PONDER 2

Consider the story starters below and then choose one to write about.

Scruffy Sam, Girl in Rags

Poor scruffy Sam. She looks so different from the other girls who come to school in their smart, freshly-ironed school uniforms. No one wants to sit next to Sam. No one lets her join in games. She gets no invitations to parties. But Sam has a secret. She's actually rich. Very, very rich. How things change when Sam's secret gets out!

The Mysterious Tola People

Deep beneath the sea live the Tola People. No one sees them. No one hears them. But when they emerge from the murky depths the Tola People see everything, they hear everything and they know everything . . . about everyone.

Rainbow of Gold

Two children hiking through the countryside see a magnificent rainbow in the distance. They make their way towards it, hoping to find the end of it. Eventually they reach the end of the rainbow, and . . . it's a pot of gold!

The Magic Football

When Marty is eleven he helps an old man who has fallen over on the pavement. The old man tells Marty (a football fan) that on his 12th birthday Marty will receive a special surprise in the post. The day comes and a package arrives addressed to 'Marty . . . Football Fan'. Inside is a magnificent golden football which Marty, after hastily gathering some of his friends, takes to the park to practise his skills. What a ball! When Marty's boot connects with it the ball unfailingly travels like a bullet to its target, bending past opponents at such speed that they are powerless to stop it.

Linda's Lucky Lantern

When the power goes off at Linda's house she remembers the lantern that her great grandfather used to speak of. It had been gathering dust in the garden shed for as long as anyone could remember. What Linda didn't know was that this was no ordinary lantern. When she lit the wick something very strange happened . . .

Magical Gaze

You wake up one morning and discover you have magical powers. By gazing at something for more than five seconds you can turn it into whatever you want . . . for an hour. The thought occurs to you that you'll be able to have some fun with your friends . . . and your enemies!

Read my Mind

You are on your way back to class when you trip over and hit your head. Ouch. Your friend picks you up.
'Are you okay?'
'Fine,' you reply.
'I didn't say anything,' your friend says.
Wow. You find you can read people's thoughts. But is it a good thing?

Tiny Friends

One quiet night, you are in the garden when you hear voices. You follow them. There are tiny people living here. And they are happy to be your friend.

Chat Cat

What if one day your cat (or dog) opened its mouth and started talking to you?

Lost in the Village of Mirrors

When the Wilson children get lost descending Mount Disappointment they follow a winding river that leads to a remote village. However, this is no ordinary village. The walls of every house and building are mirrors. Within a very short time the Wilsons are lost. Where are the villagers?

What is going on? Is there a way out or is this the beginning of an inescapable nightmare?

Magic Carpet

You're riding your bike up a steep hill. It's getting harder and harder and harder to pedal. Suddenly the chain snaps, with a sharp 'clunk'. Oh, no! But wait . . . something very strange has happened; miraculously, you're now riding on a magic carpet!

PLEASUREABLE AND PREPOSTEROUS PLOTS TO PONDER 3

Consider the story starters below and then choose one to write about.

Fishy Business

James was just about to take the fish off the hook when it spurted out, 'Eat me at your peril!'

Double Trouble

Rose and Alex are late for school. As they enter the classroom they see Mr Peters sitting at his desk in front of the class. But something must be wrong; everyone is looking at them with puzzled expressions on their faces. As they make their way to their seats they are astonished to find that their chairs are already occupied . . . by themselves!

Super Ball

Danny bounced the ball and gazed in disbelief as it bounced higher and higher and higher.

The Roller Coaster from Hell

You're on a roller coaster that's out of control. Everyone is screaming.

Down the Volcano

You and your friend are exploring the crater of an extinct volcano. You go down and down and down into the crater's depths. Your friend parts some giant ferns, peers between them and then shouts, 'Look at this . . . quickly!'

Pandora's Box

Your friend Pandora has received a mysterious box for her birthday. She calls you round to help her open it. What's inside?

Message in a Bottle

You're walking along the beach when you see a bottle that has just washed up onto the sand. It has a message in it. After carefully deciphering the faded writing you decide you'd better act fast. Really fast!

Towering Invention

You recently invented a way of getting people out of towering buildings that are on fire. This is, indeed, an amazing invention. And now's the time to try it out, for the city's tallest office block is ablaze!

Sandwiched!

You are in a restaurant and you've just been served a huge sandwich. As you're about to take a bite you hear, 'Stop, don't eat me!'

Computer Chaos

You're playing a computer game when, suddenly, all the characters in the game come to life and leap out of the screen. Oh dear, how do I stop this?

The most Terrifying Teacher

Imagine the scariest teacher alive – icy eyes, a booming voice, huge, talks like an encyclopaedia – and he/ she has just taken over your class!

Bubbles

Consider what might happen if someone invented a bubble blower that produced bubbles that could never burst.
Now write a story about it.

Magic Mirror

That new mirror you received as a present is weird. When you look in it, you can see yourself in the future. What do you see?

My Friend the Robot

You have just received the Person Plus 5000 robot as a present. Now you have a companion. But first you have to train your robot. Describe how.

ABSURDITIES 1

Choose from the titles below and see if you can come up with a fun story.

The Mouse with Boxing Gloves

The Great Dane that Chirped Like a Bird

The Camel Fashion Parade

Father Christmas, Winner of the Relay Race

The Bus Driver's a Chimpanzee!

Old Granny Cranston and her Amazing Skateboard Skills

My Cat is Half Dog!

My Teacher is an Alien!

Pigs *do* fly!

When Time ran Backwards

Additional challenge:
Can you give the story a surprise ending?

ABSURDITIES 2

Choose from the titles below and see if you can come up with a fun story.

The Elephant in the Nappy

Samuel and the Two-Metre Pizza

The Strange Little Man with a Pet Pink Alligator

The Badger Band

Living Inside a Fairy Tale

The Meowing Canary

The Singing Snail

The Yacht with the Monkey Crew

Freddie, the Boy who Hopped and Croaked Like a Frog

Talking Food

Additional challenge:
Use some direct speech (dialogue) in your story.

NATURE WILD AND WONDERFUL 1

Choose one of the natural features below and write an interesting fictional story about your experience of it.

> A towering, hollow tree

> A deep, tranquil lake

> An erupting volcano

> Crashing waves and a tall cliff

> A thundering waterfall

> A violent earthquake

> A forbidding canyon

> A forest full of butterflies

> An ancient cave in a remote place

Additional challenge:

Write in the first person. Include any **two** of the following:

- one young person apart from yourself
- a crippled old man or woman
- an animal of your choice
- a surprising ending
- some description of the scene
- a picture of an important scene

Make sure you give your story a suitable title.

NATURE WILD AND WONDERFUL 2

Two children are walking along a mountain path when a severe thunderstorm sets off a fire. As frightened animals run from the fire the children notice an injured rabbit that appears unable to escape the approaching flames.

Describe how the children rescue the rabbit, get it and themselves to safety, and soon find a person willing to adopt the rabbit as a pet.

Additional challenges:
- Your story should begin just before the thunderstorm strikes.
- Mention the names and ages of the children.
- Describe what kinds of animals are fleeing the fire.
- Use a little direct speech in your story.

OR

Two children are lost in the woods. How will they survive? How will they find their way home?

Additional challenges:
- Can you work two or more friendly animals into the story?
- Can you describe how the children ate, drank and slept while they were lost?

CURIOUS COMBINATIONS 1

Use the last three digits of your telephone number to come up with an entertaining, humorous story. You may, but don't have to, use your combination as the title.

e.g. 493: Annabelle's meeting with a curious giraffe.

Third last digit of my telephone number	Subject	Second last digit of my telephone number	Verb	Last digit of my telephone number	Animal
0	Jeremy's	0	titanic battle with a huge	0	mouse
1	Penelope's	1	encounter with an injured	1	lion cub
2	Tommy Simpson's	2	taming of a fierce	2	wolf
3	Aunty Tania's	3	wild ride on a gigantic	3	giraffe
4	Annabelle's	4	amazing hour with a howling	4	rhinoceros
5	James and Danny's	5	great adventure with a playful	5	dolphin
6	My cousin Sarah's	6	wonderful day with a friendly	6	killer whale
7	My	7	terrifying moment with a	7	seal pup
8	My grandfather's	8	crazy Sunday feeding a tiny	8	octopus
9	Mrs Abernathy's	9	meeting with a curious	9	gorilla

CURIOUS COMBINATIONS 2

Write a story based on the combination of birthday months particular to you and your family. You may (but don't have to) use your combination as the title.

My birthday month	Whose?	My Mum's birthday month	Descriptor	My Dad's birthday month	Inanimate object
Jan	Aunty May's	Jan	absolutely huge	Jan	frisbee
Feb	The Benson twins'	Feb	magical pink	Feb	refrigerator
Mar	My	Mar	ugly-looking, useless	Mar	spoon
Apr	Old Mrs Hamilton's	Apr	gigantic red	Apr	letter box
May	Uncle Tony's	May	broken-down	May	table lamp
Jun	Mr Wilson's	Jun	brand new	Jun	car
Jul	Ned the builder's	Jul	incredibly cool	Jul	bicycle
Aug	Professor Pumpernickle's	Aug	unbelievably shabby	Aug	shoes
Sep	The Alien invader's	Sep	prize-winning	Sep	chess set
Oct	Jimmy's	Oct	mysterious silver	Oct	watch
Nov	Dr Smithers'	Nov	unpredictable purple	Nov	book
Dec	Sylvia Morris's	Dec	ever-so-tiny	Dec	computer

Additional challenge:
- Can you write the story as a cartoon strip with captions?
  or
- Can you add a **fourth** item from the combinations table to your story?

STORY STARTERS 1

Here are the beginnings of some stories. Choose one and finish it.

The huge crocodile opened its jaws wide . . .

Suddenly, the sky lit up with a strange, white light . . .

The young musician walked nervously on stage . . .

A piercing scream rang out in the night . . .

A huge black bear lumbered toward the motorway . . .

I didn't believe in magic spells, but . . .

Out of the darkness and into the light of the campfire came . . .

The express train roared into the night . . .

He limped towards the waiting train . . .

Additional challenges:
- Have two main characters.
- You may make your story humorous and/ or dramatic.
- Include an animal of your choice in your story.

STORY STARTERS 2

Here are the beginnings of some stories. Choose one and finish it.

As Seeta awoke one morning from an uneasy dream she found herself transformed in her bed into a gigantic insect.

The tiny boat slowly pulled away from the shore . . .

Under a blazing hot sun an empty road stretched far into the distance . . .

The army sergeant roared . . .

Its name was Ludwig. It was huge . . .

There, right in my own back garden, was . . .

A strange smell came from the swamp. Then I heard a noise . . .

The tornado moved slowly toward our house.

I felt my body shrinking, shrinking . . .

Additional challenges:
- Have two main characters.
- You may make your story humorous and/or dramatic.
- Include an animal of your choice in your story.

STORY STARTERS 3

Here are the beginnings of some stories. Choose one and finish it.

Under the giant mushroom stood a tiny man . . .

The torch was shining directly into my tent . . .

I became more frightened with every step. . .

The ground began to sink down, down, down . . .

The strangest looking dog I've ever seen . . .

The last bar on the cage gave way, and the lion . . .

The curtains at the back of the dusty window parted slowly, and . . .

We played an odd game in which you had to . . .

All the children in the street waited anxiously . . .

Additional challenges:
- Have one main character and two supporting characters.
- One of the supporting characters is a criminal or an alien.

STORY STARTERS 4

Here are the beginnings of some stories. Choose one and finish it.

He's been missing for more than two days . . .

As the band began to play . . .

On the lid of the box was written, 'Open at your own risk' . . .

'It's arrived!' I screamed.

'Get me out of here, please!' she screamed.

Gigantic footprints led right up to the . . .

Under the pillow was a note saying . . .

Treasure!

More than anything in the world, she wanted to . . .

A penknife is the only clue to . . .

When I woke up, the wind was howling outside my window . . .

I always knew my dog was different . . .

Additional challenge:
Can you **end** your story with one of these ideas?

MENAGERIE MUSES 1

Write an entertaining story featuring *one* of these animal characters:

Trevor, the Tormented Turtle

Sasha, the Sensational Show Horse

Polly, Peter the Pirate's Particularly Pedantic Parrot

Millie, the Magic Monkey

Ollie, the Objectionable, Obnoxious Octopus

Anthony, the Amazing African Ant

Tommy and Tessa, the Twin Tabby Cats of Twyford

Daisy, the Devoted Daschund

Josh, the Jealous Jaguar

Additional challenge:
- Can you write your story as a play script? **OR**
- Can you write your story as a comic strip, with talking balloons?

MENAGERIE MUSES 2

Write an entertaining story featuring *one* of these animal characters:

Kate, the Regal Red Kite

Maggie, the Magpie who flew
to the Moon

Pippa, the Playful Penguin of
Portsmouth

Ella, the Elegant Elephant

Ali, the Weeping Alligator

Gemma, the Lonely Giraffe

Garth, the Gorgeous Gorilla

Will, the Very Wise Whale

Monty, the Magical
Mule

Olivia, the Silvery Otter

Emma, the Eagle who Eats
Easter Eggs

Additional challenge:
- Can you write your story as a play script? **OR**
- Can you write your story as a comic strip, with talking balloons?

MENAGERIE MUSES 3

Write an entertaining story featuring *one* of these animal characters:

Fred, the Giant Forest Frog

Tabitha, the Twisty, Tangly, Twitty Tarantula

Bertie, the Bee without a Buzz

Colleen, the Talking Crocodile

Jonaki, the Jubilant Jay

The Beautiful Silver Horse who Saved Miranda

The Ant that wouldn't Die

Sidney, the Slimy, Squishy-squashy Squid

Additional challenges:
- Add a second character from the list.
  OR
- Can you write the story in lines that rhyme?

MENAGERIE MUSES 4

Write an entertaining story featuring *one* of these animal characters:

Harry, the Huge Hungry Hippo

Richard, the Raucous Raven

Simon, the Sinister Spider

Holly, the Horse who Hated Hay

Samantha, the Squeamish Salamander

Fritz, the Fierce Fighting Flea

Sean, the Shambling Sheep

Dunbar, the Dim-witted Donkey

Hugh, the Happy Hedgehog

Percy, the Porky Placid Pig

Additional challenges:
- Add a second character from the list.
  OR
- Can you write the story in lines that rhyme?

ADVENTURES IN SPACE 1

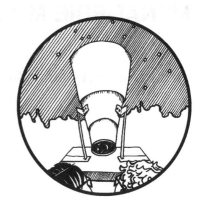

Write a story about one of the following:

Hello out there . . .

Two boy geniuses make a telescope that is so powerful that it can clearly see planets in hundreds of other solar systems.

Mission to Mars

A mission to Mars reveals something on the planet that's totally unexpected.

Astronaut Emergency

Two astronauts are on a mission. One gets injured and has to return to Earth.

Fire!

A rocket's booster jets fail to fire properly. The problem is quickly corrected by a girl prodigy at mission control.

Aliens!

A team of astronauts encounters an advanced (non-human) civilisation on Neptune.

Mirror Worlds

Two girl geniuses discover that our universe is not the only one.

> **Additional challenges:**
> * Make yourself one of the characters in the story.
> * Write in the first person.

ADVENTURES IN SPACE 2

You are part of a team of astronauts that has been sent to investigate the rings of Saturn. The team has to study the rings from very close range and, if possible, collect some of the material that makes up the rings.

Write a full account of your mission, from Blast Off to landing back on Earth. Choose from among the following complications to add suspense to your story:

You lose communication
with Earth.

A crew member gets seriously ill.

The rockets malfunction, and
have to be fixed with a 'space
walk' outside the ship.

You discover a stowaway!

You nearly get hit by a
huge asteroid.

You see something very
frightening in deep space.

Additional challenges:
- Explain what role you have on the team.
- Mention the other team members and what jobs they have to do.
- Talk about the equipment and instruments you use to retrieve, and then study, the material.
- Make mention of what you see along the way.
- Describe Saturn as your ship approaches it.

CHARISMATIC CHARACTERS 1

Write an entertaining story based on one of the characters below.

Gino the Genie

Deidre the Desert Girl

Betty the Bookworm

Mighty Matilda, the World's Strongest Girl

Extremely Embarrassing Edwin

Annoying Adam

Invisible Ian

Curious Chloe

Additional challenges:
- Devote the first paragraph to a description of your character.
- All the characters in your story have names that start with the same letter (e.g. Betty's friend might be Caroline Carter or Sylvia Smith).
- Invent a surprise ending for your story.

CHARISMATIC CHARACTERS 2

Write an entertaining story based on one of the characters below.

Babar, the Baby who Grew
and Grew and Grew

Impatient Imogene

Sparkles the Clown

Tommy the Tourist

Mrs Dillsbury, the
Wild Babysitter

Helga, the Mean and
Miserable Stepmother

Miriam, the Marvellous Musician
of Manchester

Marvin the
Marvellous Mathematician

Charles, the Cheating
Chess Player

Wendy the Waterbaby

Additional challenges:
- Devote the first paragraph to a description of your character.
- All the characters in your story have names that start with the same letter (e.g. Betty's friend might be Caroline Carter or Sylvia Smith).
- Invent a surprise ending for your story.

CHARISMATIC CHARACTERS 3

Write a fun story based on *two* of the characters below.

Rollo, the Ridiculous
Rumbling Robot

Sylvester the Disobedient Soldier

Barbara, the Girl who Blew
Huge Bubbles

Naughty Nellie, the Most
Mischievous Baby in the World

The Terrible Twins
of Twickenham

Craig, the World's
Craziest Clown

Penelope, the Princess who
Loved Pineapples

Victor the Viking

Mia the Mermaid

Tearful Toni

Puzzling Pete

CHARISMATIC CHARACTERS 4

Write a fun story based on *two* of the characters below.

Fantastic, Fearless Fred

Clumsy Clara

Mysterious Mr MacIntosh

Ace-smashing Anna

Keith, the Kindly King

George, the Gentle Giant of Gerrards Cross

Jodi, the Dolphin Girl

Hamish, the Humble Hero

Sporty Sam

Marvellous Megan

Sarah, the Girl who could Fly

John, the Jungle Boy

Old Mrs Fuss-pot

CHARISMATIC CHARACTERS 5

Write an entertaining story based on *one* of the animal characters below.

Dennis, the
Daydreaming Dinosaur

Lilly, the Loquacious Locust

Mabel, the Mischievous Mouse

Conan, the Confused Crab

Sylvia Silkworm

Charlie, the Cheeky Chimp

Willow, the Water Rat

Lorian, the Angry Ladybird

Katie, the Kamikaze Koala

Additional challenge:
• Devote the first paragraph to a description of your character.

CHARISMATIC CHARACTERS 6

Write an entertaining story based on *one* of the animal characters below.

Catherine, the Ten Metre Long Caterpillar

Veronica, the Very Vain Vole

Barry, the Bashful Badger

Arnie, the Adventurous Aardvark

Garry, the Getabout Goose

Hannah, the Hang-gliding Hippopotamus

Nichola, the Near-sighted Newt

Percy, the Poetic Pelican

Terry, the Terrified Tortoise

Kevin, the Clever Kangaroo

Elvis, the Excitable Elephant

Additional challenge:
- Devote the first paragraph to a description of your character.

CHARISMATIC CHARACTERS 7

Write a fun story based on *two* of the animal characters below.

Ryan, the Really Nice Rattlesnake

Diana, the Daredevil Dolphin

Maximillian, the Most Miserable Monkey in Mauritius

Briony, the Beautiful Butterfly

Bertie, the Bully Beetle

Peter, the Pesky Python

Anton, the Audacious Amazon Ape

Barbara the Billygoat

Erin, the Evasive Eider Duck

Bob, the Bumbling Bulldog

Ronald, the Rabid Rat

CHARISMATIC CHARACTERS 8

Write a fun story based on *two* of the animal characters below.

Sayid the Spider

Steven the Starfish

Lizzie, the Little Lost Lizard

Dudley the Dalmatian

Gracey, the
Gregarious Grasshopper

Ernie Earthworm

Candice the Crab

Tara, the Tantrum-throwing
Tiger Cub

Freddy, the Famous
Figure-skating Frog

Bumbo Bumblebee

Jerry, the Jealous Jellyfish

Mack, the Mudcrab who
invented Mud Pies

Sigmond, the Singing Seahorse

UNUSUAL PERSPECTIVES 1

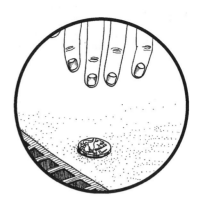

A £1 coin falls out of a woman's handbag and rolls along the pavement before settling next to a drain. The woman goes to pick it up but a young boy gets there first and walks off quickly with the coin in his hand. The agitated woman follows the boy, protesting that the coin is hers.

Imagine you are the coin. Give a first person account of what happened and where you end up.

Additional challenges:
- Describe the initial scene.
- Explain how you came into the woman's possession.
- Discuss what was with you in the woman's handbag.
- Describe how it felt when you hit the pavement.
- Mention who you would rather be with, the woman or the boy.

OR

Tell the story in a comic strip, showing every scene. Use both talking balloons and captions.

Additional challenge:
- End your story as it began.

UNUSUAL PERSPECTIVES 2

The Intruder

Setting the scene:

Seven tiny balls of fluff lay motionless in a basket. A soft, occasional 'miaow' from the proud mother is all that can be heard. Then, out of nowhere, an ominous dark shadow looms . . .

Write this story from beginning to end.

Additional instructions:

- Write from the point of view of the intruder.
- Write in the first person.
- Do not include any humans in your story.
- Use at least six adjectives (describing words).
- Use at least two adverbs to describe your movements (e.g. *silently*).

OR

Seven tiny balls of fluff lay motionless in a basket. A soft, occasional 'miaow' from the proud mother is all that can be heard. Then a child's hand reaches into the basket. 'Hello, Kitty', it says.

Write what happens next.

Additional instructions:

- Invent a dramatic surprise.
- Make sure the story ends nicely.

FABULOUS AND FANCIFUL FASHIONS 1

Write a story with one of the titles below:

My Father's Embarrassing Tie

Alison's Fluorescent Green Tracksuit

Rose's Remarkable Green Trainers

Susan's Squeaky Shoes

Tommy and the Huge Black Sandals

Laura's Lost Leotards

The Propellor Hat

See-through Shoes

Additional challenges:
- Mention where the person got their clothing item.
- Describe what happenend:
  - did it get stolen?
  - did it cause a stir?
  - did it have special powers?
  - did it annoy anyone?
  - did everyone want one too?
- Explain what happened to this fanciful fashion item in the end.

FABULOUS AND FANCIFUL FASHIONS 2

Write a story with _one_ of these titles:

The Hat that was much Too Big

The Missing Purple Sock

The Girl in Silver Overalls

Georgia Gladbury's Gloves

The Man in the Pink and Green Suit

Scary Seth and his Studded Motorcycle Jacket

The Boy with Flying Shoes

The Chameleon Suit (it changes colour wherever you go)

Mrs Periwinkle's Pink Pantaloons

Jeremiah's New Tie

Additional challenges:
* Your story involves a main character and a neighbour.
* Include at least two emotion/feeling words (e.g. anger, pleasure).
* Have a surprise ending.
* Work a proverb or 'moral' into the story – preferably to end with.

SINISTER SCALLYWAGS, VEXATIOUS VILLAINS, ROGUES AND RASCALS 1

Ronnie Rascal, a bank robber who has managed to elude police for ten years, is finally caught in the act. Describe how Ronnie comes to grief as he attempts to enter the bank through the roof and accidentally sets off the alarm.

Additional challenges:

*   Devote your entire first paragraph to a description of Ronnie Rascal. A typical sentence could be *A long, ugly scar ran from just under his right eye to his gaunt and whiskery left cheek.*
    OR
*   Write a story featuring Ronnie's mates – all scoundrels. Choose one from each list below.

Lawless Laura	Peter the Pest	Harold the Hacker
Charlie the Cheat	Claude the Fraud	Light-fingered Luke
Roger the Rogue	Stella the Stealer	Larry the Liar
Willy the Weasel	Phil the Fibber	Freddie the Firestarter
Pilfering Penelope	Sharon the Shoplifter	Henry the Hoaxer
Nancy the Nuisance	Percy the Pickpocket	Vinnie the Villain
Robber Reggie	Julia the Jewel Thief	Penny the Purse Pincher
Fighting Frank	Jailbird Jack	Dynamite Di
Calvin the Con	Randal the Vandal	Safe-cracking Sam
Syd the Snatcher	Violent Violet	Cunning Clive
Slimy Cyril	Graffiti Graham	Filthy Fran
Cathy the Cat Burglar	Raiding Rafiq	Colin the Counterfeit
Disappearing Dennis	Whiskers Wilson	Midnight Mary
Carl the Car Thief	Window-smashing Will	

SINISTER SCALLYWAGS, VEXATIOUS VILLAINS, ROGUES AND RASCALS 2

Make up a story featuring any *two* of the following:

Sly Silverfish, the World's Most Wanted Woman, a perfectionist at picking people's pockets

The Marauding Mob of Marylebone

Brutus Baddingham, the Biggest Bully in Belgravia

'Diamonds' Debbie, the Jewel Grabber

Littering Leo, the Lazy Lad of Llandudno

Tania and Terence, the Terrible Teens of Tipperary

Slimy Seth, the slickest thief in downtown New York

Friday Freda, a felon who fleeces folk only on Fridays

Theresa, the Train Terroriser

Horrible Hannah the Hellraiser

Ewan the Explosives Expert

OR
Two colourful scallywags of your own invention

Additional challenge:
Create a 'Wanted' poster for your two scoundrels.

IF I COULD 1

**Choose one of the following and
write about a day in your life:**

If I could . . .

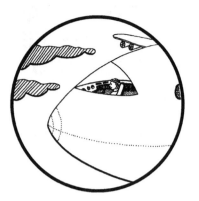

Pilot a jumbo jet

Write to a person I admire

Have three wishes

Be leader of my country

Swim and breathe underwater
like a fish

Invent something
terribly important

Do one thing to benefit
our planet

Go back in time

Read others' minds

See into the future

Travel wherever I wanted to

IF I COULD 2

Choose one of the following and write about a day in your life:

If I could . . .

Be any age I wanted

Invent a new toy

Be someone else for a day

Be any animal I choose

Run like a cheetah

Buy whatever I wanted

Perform magic

Be a sporting superstar

Spin a web like a spider

Choose my career now

Fly like a bird

Be a famous musician

Become invisible

IF I COULD 3

Choose one of the following and write about a day in your life:

If I could . . .

Be a baby again

Save any animal from extinction

Build the world's biggest kite

Eat what I liked for a day

Live in the house of my dreams

Have my own private robot

Sail around the world

Make people laugh

Make someone happy

Improve one thing about myself

Visit a planet

IF I COULD 4

Choose one of the following and write about a day in your life:

If I could . . .

Rule Earth for a year

Sit high up in a tree for a day

Be any animal I choose for a day

Be a famous chef

Be a famous writer

Be famous for one thing

Remember everything

Be captain of a sailing ship

Be a whale

Be a circus clown

Be a famous explorer

Invent a new game

Be three metres tall

MYRIAD OF MIXES 1

Starting from the left, choose a
word from each list to make a title.
Then write an entertaining story
based on that title.

Whose	Adjective 1	Adjective 2	Object
Grandma's	Wonderful	Silver	Coin
Dr Greg's	Unique	Bronze	Trophy
Mrs Mayberry's	Unusual	Antique	Watch
Jimmy Wilson's	Tiny	Gold	Dish

Additional challenges:
- Can you write the story as a play script?
  OR
- Can you think of a surprise ending?

MYRIAD OF MIXES 2

Write an entertaining story by first obtaining (using your three initials) the setting, the subject and a featured object from the grid below.

My first initial	Setting	My middle initial	Whom	My last initial	Object
A	In a dingy basement	A	Mr Smith	A	an antique grandfather clock
B	Standing in a public park	B	Professor Blumen-feld's spoilt niece	B	a huge yellow mushroom
C	Out at sea in a furious storm	C	Father Christmas	C	a small candle
D	On my uncle's dairy farm	D	Mr and Mrs Pope	D	an invisible hand-held alarm
E	Zooming through space	E	Samuel Welstead	E	a mouse trap
F	In the city at lunchtime	F	The village postman	F	a water pistol
G	In the middle of a lovely meadow	G	Tiny Mrs Peters	G	a shiny new pen
H	At the shopping centre	H	Lazy Bob	H	a broken stapler
I	Inside a crater on the moon	I	Wendy the bookworm	I	a tiny radio
J	In a dirty, smelly lane at night	J	Mrs Webster's baby	J	a small silver key
K	In a bakery	K	Mary-Jane and her friend Kate	K	an extremely old coin
L	On the east side of an erupting volcano	L	Old Grumble Bones	L	a powerful torch
M	Floating on a cloud	M	Max the muscleman	M	a small wooden box
N	In the florist shop	N	Harry the world's fastest man	N	a huge black ball
O	In a nuclear-powered submarine	O	Laughing Larry	O	a smart new watch
P	On a tropical island	P	Jack Stokes, the richest boy in town	P	a pair of spectacles
Q	At the local library	Q	Bozo the clown	Q	a tiny pebble
R	At the annual fair	R	Gracey Gordon, the girl with golden hair	R	a wallet stuffed with money
S	Rowing a canoe on the lake	S	Scarlet the sculptor	S	a large red button
T	In the bathroom	T	Pinnochio	T	a set of false teeth
U	Sitting at my school desk	U	Wenzel, the wonderful wizard	U	a broken shoe
V	On one of the rides in Disneyland	V	Prunella the Princess	V	a floppy disk
W	In the Swiss Alps	W	Oscar, the crazy scientist	W	a treasure chest
X	Down by the river	X	Johnny the dustman	X	a ball of wool
Y	On an aeroplane	Y	Susie the star	Y	a hard-to-read map
Z	Climbing up a mountain	Z	Mr and Mrs Potts	Z	a magic potion

STICKY SITUATIONS 1

Continue one of these stories, giving it a happy ending.

Peanut Buttered

I wish Dad wouldn't fool around with his pointless inventions! His amazing Shrink Machine was just the last straw. Now look at me. My horrible little brother Rodney has put me inside a jar of peanut butter. What can I do?

The Banana

I'm a banana. I don't mind being peeled and then eaten in the usual way. It's just the thought of being cut up into little pieces. I'm lying helplessly in a glass bowl on a kitchen counter top. Oh, no, here she comes . . . with a sharp knife. She picks me up in her left hand and begins to peel me. What can I do?

The Ferris Wheel

I'm a ferris wheel. I love giving people rides, especially children. Now my owners are saying I'm too old and they're talking about dismantling me and sending me to the scrap heap. And now it looks like my time has come . . . I can see two men walking towards me; each is carrying a large spanner.

Nightie Fright

I just went outside to check on Fido the dog, who was howling. But the door slammed shut on me. Now I can't get back inside, and no one's at home. Here I am, in the back garden, wearing nothing but my nightie!

STICKY SITUATIONS 2

Imagine you're in one of the situations below. Write the story of how you miraculously get to safety. Give your story a suitable title.

Half-way through a bungee jump, you see two starving lions waiting at the bottom.

Stranded on top of a skyscraper in the middle of an earthquake.

In a swamp with starving crocodiles.

On an expedition looking at a tomb of a mummy. The mummy breaks through the lid.

In a glass dome two kilometres under the sea when the glass starts to crack.

Climbing a mountain with nothing to hang on to. Your rope starts to break.

In a space station with others when the oxygen starts to run out.

In a rubber dinghy in the middle of the Pacific Ocean. A shark is next to the dinghy and the dinghy is losing air.

Stranded in the middle of a blistering hot desert with no water to drink.

Stuck in the crater of a volcano that is about to erupt.

Walking in the desert. Your camels have run off with all the food and water supplies.

Flying across the Atlantic Ocean in a light aircraft, your pilot suddenly collapses at the wheel.

Swimming in the ocean, a massive wave pulls you out to sea.

TANTALISING TITLES 1

Choose any title and write an entertaining story.

Crocodile! My Narrow Escape

The Time Machine

The Girl who Tamed a Tiger

The Pair of Shoes with Talking Tongues

Anaconda Attack

The Juggling Spider

Barking Frogs and Croaking Dogs

House of Treasures

The Horse that Didn't Belong Anywhere

Bound for Jupiter

Invasion of the Giant Insects

The Plant that Grew and Grew and Grew

The Sneeze that Caused a Tidal Wave

Simone's Secret Hideaway

TANTALISING TITLES 2

Choose any title and write an entertaining story.

Oasis in the Desert

Miraculous Matthew's Mission

Lost in a Cave

Lonely Mr Smithers

My Friend Alf

Mystery of the White Pony

The Magician

The Amazing Dancing Shoes

The Wonderful World of Walter the Wizard

Revenge of the Creepy Crawlies

Timothy's Amazing Telescope

Danny and the Valley of Mysteries

Molly's Mysterious Message

Planet out of Control

My Very Embarrassing Brother

Winston's Woeful Wednesday

My Unforgettable Dream

Jealous Julia

TANTALISING TITLES 3

Choose any title and write an entertaining story.

Riddle of the Lost City

The Wicked Witch from Wimbledon

Runaway Bus!

The Day the Sun Fell out of the Sky

The Elephant that Lost its Trunk

Ride on an Iceberg

The Sad Snowman

The Boy who Lived in a Tree

The Bouncy Bubble that No-one Could Burst

The Day the Headmaster Trod in My Chewing Gum

Revenge of the Million Fleas

Sensational Sally's Super Saturday

Sarah's Grandfather Clock

Robert's Remarkable Recipe

TANTALISING TITLES 4

Choose any title and write an entertaining story.

Mystery of the
Never-ending Train

The Bowling Giraffe

The Boy who could Read Minds

The Woman Who Sneezed and
Blew Down Houses

The Man with the Magic
Walking Stick

Ulysses, the Magnificent Unicorn

The Kind-Hearted Gorilla

Amazon Adventure

The Woman with Laser Eyes

Mandy's Magic Mirror

The Worst Day of My Life

The Golden Swan

The Little Old Man and his
Pet Tiger

The Winged Dog

The Little Old Lady with Green
Spiky Hair

The Star that couldn't Shine

The Silver Seal

Drums in the Night

PERKY PETS 1

Choose an idea and write a story from a pet's point of view.

The Leaking Bowl

My name is Goldie the Goldfish. I have a problem. My bowl is leaking. The little boy who owns me thinks he fixed it by putting plasters on the bowl. But it's still leaking . . .

Sylvia the Snake

Why do people find us snakes frightening? We just want the quiet life – up a tree or down a hole. But even when a little boy bought me and I found myself a 'pet' – I was forever giving someone a shock. Here's how . . .

The Cunning Cat

Hi, I'm Chloe the Cat. My humans think they control me. But actually *I* control *them*. Want to know how?

Terry the Troublesome Terrier

My name is Terry. I'm a terrier. I'm fast. I'm excitable. I'm . . . always getting into trouble. Let me tell you about it.

Horace the High-spirited Horse

I'm Horace the Horse. I belong to a riding school. The trouble is, I don't like riders. They're too nervous, or too confident, or too noisy, or too silent. I like to have fun with them. Let me tell you how.

Percy the Parrot

I'm Percy. I can talk not just parrot talk – human talk! And I have great fun adding my bit to human conversations I overhear. I'll give you some examples.

PERKY PETS 2

Choose an idea and write a story from a pet's point of view.

A guard dog who's afraid of mice

A cat who thinks her owners are strange

A farm boy who always goes fishing with his pet goat

A bird who shares secrets with the family cat

A girl who rides across the country on her horse

A woman who puts her baby elephant to bed each night

A pirate's parrot

A pet-shop owner who talks to the animals about the customers

A woman whose best friend is her pet giraffe

A girl whose pet cat is in love with a dog

A boy whose dog has an amazing appetite

A girl who takes her pet pig to school one day

A woman who lives with 100 cats

Additional challenge:
Write the story from the owner's point of view

GHOSTLY, GHOULISH AND GHASTLY 1

Write a story about a graveyard at midnight. Here are some story ideas.

The Friendly Ghost

A family of ghosts lives in the graveyard. One of the young ghosts likes humans and wants to be their friend. This ghost doesn't like scaring people. However . . .

Dare Scare

Three children have dared one another to spend the night in the graveyard. What they don't know is that another friend is dressed up as a ghost, and he's coming too.

Ghost Party

It's midnight on Halloween. All the ghosts come out to play. Heaven help any mortal who comes by.

'Rob, is that you?'

Tom is celebrating his ninth birthday by camping in a tent down at the old graveyard with two of his best friends. They begin to tell ghost stories. Suddenly, something rustles in the bushes. Has one of the ghosts come to haunt the boys, or is it just Tom's older brother, Rob?

> **Additional challenges:**
> * Create an eerie atmosphere, with slow-moving mist.
> * There is the crack of lightning and the rumble of thunder.
> * There is a hooting owl.

GHOSTLY, GHOULISH
AND GHASTLY 2

Write a story entitled *Ghoulish Gourmet.*

Additional challenges:
- The ghosts are planning a boo-b-que.
- Give all the food ghostly names. Suggestions are: RIP tomb-atoes, spirit soup, graveyard gravy, screeches of sauce, spooky spices, clanging cloves, ghosts' roast on toast, howls of herbs, horror hamburgers, scary stew, frightening fritters.
- The story sequence is: organising the boo-b-que, the boo-b-que itself and then the ghosts returning to their homes in the village graveyard.
- If you decide to single out a few characters in your story give them ghostly names.

OR

Write a story entitled *Revenge of the Sorrowful Spook.*

Additional challenges:
- The sorrowful spook has to get revenge on someone.
- No violence please – just lots of scaring.
- Can you tell the story so that it ends with a surprise?
- What happened to the sorrowful spook to make him/her so sad?

SEA AND SKY 1

Choose one of these and write the story.

Eat Me

You are enjoying your adventure in a hot-air balloon when suddenly you get blown off course and land on an island inhabited by cannibals.

Fishy Friends

Ollie the Octopus and Sharon the Squid form a romantic attachment. Their families don't approve and so they decide to elope.

Here in the Sphere

You are a scientist living at the bottom of the sea in a glass sphere. You are studying fish and marine plants. All goes well until one day you lose contact with the surface. What happens next?

Robinson Caruso

You are the only survivor of a shipwreck. You find yourself on a deserted island. However, there's plenty of plant and animal life. What will you do while you wait to be rescued?

Castle in the Clouds

Sarah spends hours looking through her telescope up into the clouds. One day, she discovers that there is a castle amongst the clouds. Who lives there? How can Sarah fly up there to find out?

Eagle Eye

Mervin is a very small boy who owns a very big pet eagle. Every night, the eagle lets Mervin climb onto its back so they can fly away into the night for exciting adventures.

SEA AND SKY 2

Earthquake!

A powerful earthquake triggers a massive tidal wave off the coast of Peru. As the tsunami races towards the mainland, millions flee to the hills and mountains. Then something miraculous happens.

Decide what happens and then tell the whole story.

> Possible Scenarios:
> - A superhero saves the day.
> - Another earthquake sends shockwaves in the opposite direction, neutralising the tsunami.

OR

Fly like a Bird

Your uncle Ned invented a 'Birdy Backpack'. When you strap it on you can fly like a bird. It's perfectly safe. Now, what will you do with it?

> Additional challenges:
> - The Birdy Backpack has only one fault Uncle Ned didn't tell you about.
> - Your Mum hears about the Birdy Backpack and sets out to bring you down to earth.
> - Mike Mantle, the meanest boy at school, sees you flying with the backpack and tries everything he can to steal it from you.
> - Uncle Ned was so happy with his flying backpack idea that he has invented a 'Fishy Backpack' that lets you swim and breathe underwater!

DELIGHTFUL AND DELICIOUS DELICACIES 1

A Fantastic Food Find

Write a story about the time you found a diamond wedding ring in something you were eating. The ring has a telephone number engraved inside and you receive a £1,000,000 reward from its grateful and very wealthy owner.

> **Additional challenges:**
> - Provide a graphic description of your meal, e.g. *The pizza looked delicious, with a covering of strips of ham, a ring of juicy pineapple pieces, mouth-watering olives, fresh mushrooms, bright green peppers and fleshy tomato.*
> - Give a good description (physical and character) of the ring's owner.

OR

The Chocolate Funpark

Willie Wonka has opened a Chocolate Funpark – like Disneyland – and you have just received an invitation to visit.

> **Additional challenges:**
> - Can you find a way to 'sample' all the rides?
> - At the end – do you love chocolate more, or have you given it up for life?
> - Describe the funpark in detail – what does it look like? Taste like? Smell like? Sound like? Feel like?

DELIGHTFUL AND DELICIOUS DELICACIES 2

Birthday Banquet

Cheri the Chef is asked to prepare a sumptuous meal for you and your family and relatives, a total of 32 people. As it's your birthday you get to decide the menu. Tell the story of how Cheri, after numerous frustrations, finally manages to prepare all the courses in time for the 1 o'clock feast.

> **Additional challenges:**
> - Begin with this sentence: *I tell Cheri that for the starter I would like baby prawns dipped in Italian sauce.*
> - Give Cheri clear instructions, e.g. *Then I tell her that for dessert I'd like a huge cake with 2 cm of cream in the middle and a layer of banana icing on top.*
> - Include this sentence or something like it: *Cheri begins to panic and races to the kitchen to check her supplies of potatoes, almost tripping over a chair on the way.*

OR

The Wonderbar

You have just invented a marvellous new edible delicacy that combines the taste of chocolate, the fizz of lemonade, the aroma of strawberry jam and the feel of ice-cream. You call it the 'Wonderbar'. Write an advert for it, then tell the story of how it conquered the world.

> **Additional challenges:**
> - It comes in strange shapes and sizes.
> - It is a health food as well.
> - The Wonderbar is so successful that you launch into a wide range of related products, such as Wondersludge (a smoothie) and Wondercups (lunchbox-sized cup cakes).
> - A dentist claims the Wonder products cause tooth decay. You have to prove him wrong.

WORLD OF WIZARDRY, WICKED WITCHES AND MAGIC 1

Choose a title and write a story full of action, mystery, spooks and surprises.

Sam's Amazing Crystal Ball

The Witch of Cliff-top Lighthouse

The Dungeon of Rats

The Strange Rat-Cat of Misty Hollow

Bats, Owls and other Creatures of the Night

Wally, the Wand-less Wizard

Penelope's Potion

Sinister Susan and her Seven Secret Spells

Old Mrs Haggard and her Wicked Brew

The Castle on Magic Mountain

WORLD OF WIZARDRY, WICKED WITCHES AND MAGIC 2

Choose a title and write a story full of action, mystery, spooks and surprises.

The Valley of Bats

Walter the Wand Maker

Simon's Secret Spell

The Land of the Invisible People

The Black Cat of Oldham Castle

The Revenge of the Rats

Susannah and the Spell that Saved the World

Cassie and the Eternally Boiling Cauldron

The Wizard of Golem Gorge

Olivia's Owl

Norse, the Jet Black Horse

Wizz Fizz, the Little Learning Witch

The Cat with Nine Hundred Lives

FAIRIES AND FANTASIES 1

Write a story based on one of the ideas below.

Fairy Friends

There are fairies at the bottom of the garden. And they are your friends. Tell of your adventures together.

Ursula and her Unicorn

Ursula was walking in the forest one day when she came upon a unicorn. The unicorn was in trouble, so Ursula helped it out. It became her very good friend. What happened next?

O'Leary the Leprechaun

On your visit to Ireland, you came upon a leprechaun. You know the story – leprechauns know the way to a hidden pot of gold. Well, what happened?

Dudley the Dragon

Everyone is scared of dragons – but *you*. That's because your dragon is a sweetie. His name is Dudley – and he flies.

Emmeline the Elf and Misty Moonlight

Emmeline is a tiny elf who lives in a hollow toadstool in the middle of an enchanted forest. Her best friend is her fairy horse, Misty Moonlight. Together, they help save the enchanted forest from being cut to the ground.

When the World fell Asleep

Asher woke up in her normal bed, in a normal town and got ready for a normal day at school. Little did she know that she would be the only person awake. The whole world had fallen asleep.

FAIRIES AND FANTASIES 2

Write a story based on one of the ideas below.

Toy Talk

You wake up one night to the sound of whispering. You open one eye. The toys are talking to one another. What do they say?

Thumbelina

In the garden is a flower. In the flower is a tiny person. Her name is Thumbelina.

Rumpelstiltskin's Really Nice Brother

The miller's daughter tricked Rumpelstiltskin, by finding out his name. Thank goodness, because he was a real meanie. But his brother, Rory, is a lovely little gnome. Tell the story of the help he gave another, much nicer, girl.

Norman the Gnome

Gnomes live in underground houses. They only come out at night. One gnome, called Norman, is accident prone. He is often nearly caught by a curious human. Tell the story of one of Norman's near misses.

Fidget Fairy

Fidget is a little fairy who just can't sit still. At fairy school, she fidgets, at home she fidgets and even when she's asleep she fidgets. One afternoon, Fidget was out in the grassy clearing in the middle of the forest, bouncing around as usual, when a huge, sniffing dog came running up behind her. Fidget flew into a hollow stump but the dog came sniffing after her. Will her fidgeting ways get her in trouble?

Fireflies Galore

It is a beautiful, summery night and you are lying on your trampoline looking up at the sky. Suddenly, little flashes of light rush past your eyes. It is a flock of fireflies. You jump up and follow them. Where do you end up?

MARVELLOUS
MUSIC 1

Write a great story with one of these titles.

Gavin's Guitar

The Baby who played the Piano

Mitch and the Missing Melody

Mr Bertram and his
Brilliant Band

The Singer who Lost her Voice

Sara and the Soothing Harp

Little Joe and the
Double Bass

The Golden Sounds of
Vicky's Violin

Abbey, the Girl with the
Golden Flute

Robert's Trombone

Kerrie's Keyboard

MARVELLOUS MUSIC 2

Write a great story with one of these titles.

The Crazy Conductor
of Colchester

Gayle and the Golden Trumpet

The Choir that Conquered
the World

The Lost Violin

Curious Chris and the
Red Clarinet

The Piano that Played by Itself

The Humming Blade of Grass

Fiona, the Formidable Flautist

Dora's Darstardly Drum Kit

Olga's 'Orrible Oboe

Ben's Banjo

Zelda's Xylophone

The Bluesy Bass Guitar

JOURNEYS FAR AND WIDE 1

Here are some titles for an adventure story. Choose one and write the story as a first person account (you are the central character).

Sailing on the High Seas

Mission to Pluto

Marty's Supersonic Experience

Mountain Adventure

Fiona's Journey to Freedom

Voyage to the South Pole

Journey through the Lost World of Altantis

Desert Trek

Additional challenges:

- Describe how you prepared for your trip.
- Who went with you?
- Include a near mishap (e.g. a violent storm, accident, etc.).
- Who or what did you encounter on your journey?
- What supplies did you take?
- Were you in radio contact with anyone?
- Did you need to take special clothing?
- What, if anything, did you learn?

JOURNEYS FAR AND WIDE 2

Here are some titles for an adventure story. Choose one and write the story as a first person account (you are the central character).

Living in the Treetops

Journey to the Bottom of the Sea

African Jungle Adventure

On Safari

Around the World in a Hot-air Balloon

Admirable Adam's Amazonian Adventure

Mountain Explorer

Tunnelling into the Earth's Core

Trip to the Edge of the Universe

Additional challenges:
- Describe how you prepared for your trip.
- Who went with you?
- What supplies did you take?
- Did you need to take special clothing?
- Were you in radio contact with anyone?
- Include a near mishap (e.g. violent storm, accident, etc.).
- Who or what did you encounter on your journey?
- What did you learn?

SENSATIONAL SETTINGS 1

Create a story to go with one of these settings.

In a Dream

Under a Mushroom

A Spider's Web

At a Festival

At the Airport

At a Carnival

A Hidden Valley

At the Bottom of a Waterfall

On a Cloud

Amongst the Stars

A Forbidden Forest of Bats and Owls

The Desert at Sunrise

Riding a Huge Wave in Hawaii

At a Fair

A Quiet Library

At the Zoo

At the Circus

On an Iceberg

In the Land of Giants

A School of Secrets

SENSATIONAL SETTINGS 2

Create a story to go with one of these settings.

In the Bathroom

At the Post Office

At the Railway Station

In the Deep Dark Jungle during the Middle of the Night

On my Bike

On the Rocks

On a Theatre Stage

In the Rain

On the Surface of the Moon

On a Jetty

In the Dark Forest

Under a Tree

In a Zooming Rocket

In my Drawer

In an Office

In a Time Machine

In a Black Cave on the Bottom of the Sea

In the Emperor's Palace

At a Barbecue

In a Busy City

On a Speeding Train

1,000 Metres Deep Underwater with the Sea Creatures

On Granddad's Farm

In a Helicopter

Near a Quiet Stream

In a Very Tall Tree

SENSATIONAL SETTINGS 3

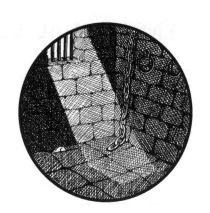

Create a story to go with one of these settings.

In a Dark Dungeon

In the Garden

Riding on a Woolly Mammoth in the Ice Age

In the Country

At the Butcher's

In a Skyscraper

In a Restaurant

On an Island

In a Church, Temple or Mosque

At the Swimming Pool

In a Very Old House

On a Shaky Bridge

On a Green Leaf

Under my Bed

Sliding on a Blood Cell inside a Human Body

At a Shopping Centre

In a Haunted House

On a Horse

Near the North Pole

Floating on an Iceberg

In a Submarine

At the Park

SENSATIONAL SETTINGS 4

Create a story to go with one of these settings.

In a Dark and Dingy Basement

Bungee Jumping

In a Speed Boat

Under a Parachute

In a Tree House

Inside a Crystal Ball

At a Scary Movie

In a Beehive

At a Fancy Dress Party

At Grandma's House

In a Dinosaur Park

At Halloween

In Hospital

Up in the Attic

At a Cemetery

In a Runaway Car

In the Laundry

In an Igloo

In a Lion's Den

In the Titanic at the Bottom of the Sea

Looking at an Egyptian Pyramid

Additional challenges:
- Combine **two** or more settings in one story.
- Write the story as a play.
- Write the story as a news report.
- Draw the setting and write the story as notes on various parts of a picture.

FEARLESS FRIENDS AND FORMIDABLE FOES 1

Scary!

Try to think of the most fearsome person or animal you can. This person/animal may be real or fictitious. Now think up a character who rescues you from this fearsome foe. Tell the whole story.

Additional challenges:

- Begin with a peaceful setting.
- Gradually change the mood from peaceful to eerie/uncertain.
- Introduce your enemy, suddenly and dramatically.
- You soon find yourself in a perilous predicament.
- Your mystery friend comes to your aid.

OR

Humorous Horror

Take a scary book or movie you have seen and rewrite it as **comedy**. You might change the villains to softies, or mix different stories together, or create jokes and puns based on horror.

FEARLESS FRIENDS AND FORMIDABLE FOES 2

Choose one of the titles below. Then write a story about your encounter with the title's subject.

The Crocodile of Misty Swamp

The Face at the Window

The Glob from Golem Street Drain

The Night I met a Werewolf

The Ghost of Nether Valley

The Starving Pack of Wolves

The Cannibals of Kalimantan

Mike the Murderous Pirate

Dracula Lives!

The Thing under My Bed

Boogyman Goes Beserk

The Green Goop from the Dark Underground Basement

Dr Evil Lurks in the Shadows of your Cupboard

SLEEPING AND DREAMING 1

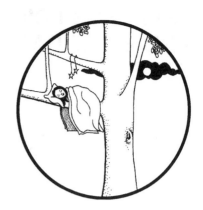

Write an amusing story about any one of these:

A girl who sleeps in a tree

A teacher who sleeps in class

A dream that turns out to be reality

A woman who sleeps with a fully grown python on her bed

A man whose snoring wakes up the next town

A boy who slept for two years

A man who sleep-walks through the city

A girl who sleeps with her eyes open

A dream that is a prophecy

When I dreamt that I was an ant

A boy who sleeps standing up

SLEEPING AND DREAMING 2

Write an amusing story about any one of these:

Mrs Parker, who dreamt she was a baby

A boy who dreamt he discovered a treasure chest

A teacher who dreamt she had the world's worst class

A boy who dreams he is Father Christmas

A woman who dreamt she was stealing from supermarket shelves

A girl who dreams she is a supermodel

A man who dreamt he was trapped in the jaws of a Tyrannosaurus Rex

A girl who dreams she is a horse

A boy who dreams he is a dog

Mr Simpson, who dreamt he was an acrobat

The boy who was afraid to go to sleep

Mrs Baxter's case of sleep-talking

Boris, the baby who slept and slept

WONDERFUL WORLD OF SCIENCE 1

Write a story based on one of these ideas:

Voyage to the Centre of the Body

You and your fellow scientists are on board a miniature submarine sent to fix a problem in an important person's body. Tell the story.

OR

What if . . .?

- What if people could be cloned?
- What if time travel was really possible?
- What if someone successfully developed 'teleporting' ('Beam me up, Scottie')
- What if someone developed a miracle cure for all diseases?
- What if you could buy invisibility paint?
- What if lost memories could be read from the brain like a movie?
- What if a scientist developed a way to breed dogs that walk on two legs?
- What if it was discovered that humans could fly by using pure concentration?
- What if two people had a conversation in their dreams that they both remembered when they woke?

WONDERFUL WORLD OF SCIENCE 2

Write a story with one of these titles:

William the Weatherman

Mile's Magnificent Magnet

Elizabeth's Exciting Experiment

Gavin and the Zero Gravity Machine

Geoff, the Genius Geologist

The Incredible World of Silvester the Scientist

Katie's Curious Chemical Concoction

Sally and her Powerful Microscope

Brittney, the Biologist

Albert's Daring Experiment and its Remarkable Outcome

Sebastian's Scientific Secret

Diana's Dinosaur Discovery

Elvin, the Electronics Whiz

Phil, the Fabulous Physicist

MYTHS AND MYSTERIES 1

Write a wonderful story entitled
Valley of the Unicorns.

Additional challenges:
- Include a human character who accidentally discovers the hidden valley of unicorns.
- Have one unicorn who is the leader of the herd.
- Your story tells how the unicorns save the person from the peril of an an impending avalanche.
- The grateful person befriends the unicorns and, accompanied by a friend, visits them often, being careful to keep the whereabouts of their valley a secret.

OR

Write any one of the following characters into a completely new story:

- Hercules
- Robin Hood
- King Arthur
- Joan of Arc
- Sir Lancelot
- William Tell
- The Bogeyman
- Tinkerbell

MYTHS AND MYSTERIES 2

Sometime, somewhere, someone had a dream.
Write the story of that dream after choosing from one of these titles.

Little Lonnie, the
Green Leprechaun

Danny finds the Dragon's Lair

Cave of the Cyclops

Howl of the Werewolf

Miriam, the Golden
Haired Mermaid

The Knight with the Silver Sword

The Phoenix and the Lost City
of Nivarna

The Fairy King

Goblins for Hire

The Elf and the Crystal

Additional challenges:
- At the end, link the dream to something real in your life (e.g. a toy or memory).
- Do *not* finish with: 'It was all a dream.'

A FINAL FEW

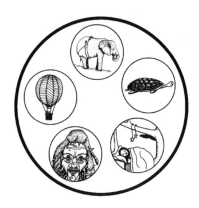

Make a Myth

- How did the ostrich come to walk instead of fly?
- Why do moles live in holes?
- Why does a cockatoo have a crest that shoots up like a flag?

Provide the answers to questions like these in story form.

Fracture a Fairy Tale

- What would happen if Goldilocks made friends with the bears?
- Or if the wolf was scared of Red Riding Hood?
- Or if you mixed two completely different fairy tales together?

Mangle a Movie

Everyone likes movie stories. Take one that was so bad it made you laugh, and rearrange it or exaggerate it to make fun of it.

Hypothetical History

- What if the Captain of the Titanic had seen the iceberg earlier?
- What if Captain Cook had missed Australia?
- What if the dinosaurs had not become extinct?

Tell the story.